THE GHOST FILES

GHOST HUNTERS

by Michael Martin

Consultant:
Dr. Andrew Nichols
Director
American Institute of Parapsychology
Gainesville, Florida

CAPSTONE PRESS
a capstone imprint

Edge Books are published by Capstone Press,
1710 Roe Crest Drive, North Mankato, Minnesota 56003.
www.capstonepub.com

Books published by Capstone Press are manufactured with paper
containing at least 10 percent post-consumer waste.

Library of Congress Cataloging-in-Publication Data
Martin, Michael, 1948–
   Ghost hunters / By Michael Martin.
   p. cm.—(Edge books. The Ghost Files)
   Includes bibliographical references and index.
   Summary: "Describes the different methods, techniques, and tools used
by ghost hunters, and relates stories about some ghost hunters' experiences"—
Provided by publisher.
   ISBN 978-1-4296-6517-9 (library binding)
   1. Ghosts—Research—Juvenile literature. I. Title. II. Series.
BF1471.M37 2012
133.1072—dc22
                                          2011003787

Editorial Credits
Aaron Sautter, editor; Tracy Davies, designer; Svetlana Zhurkin,
     media researcher; Eric Manske, production specialist

Photo Credits
Alamy: Beepstock/Robin Beckham, 5; AP Photo: Stephen Morton, 27;
Courtesy of L'Aura Hladik, 23; The Friedrich Jürgenson Foundation,
15; Getty Images: Steve and Donna O'Meara, 11; Landov: MCT
Kimberly P. Mitchell, cover, Reuters/Jessica Rinaldi, 29; Newscom:
KRT/J. Albert Diaz, 9, MCT/Barbara Nitke, 25, PacificCoastNews/James
Breeden, 13, 21, ZUMA Press/Kayte Deioma, 17, 19, ZUMA Press/o44,
7; Rex USA: Everett/Sci-Fi, 26

Printed in the United States of America in Stevens Point, Wisconsin.
092011   006391R

TABLE OF CONTENTS

Chapter 1: Ghostly Mysteries 4

Chapter 2: Ghost Hunting Tools 8

Chapter 3: Going on the Hunt 16

Chapter 4: Hunter Tales 22

Glossary 30

Read More 31

Internet Sites 31

Index 32

GHOSTLY MYSTERIES

It's a dark night and you're home alone. Suddenly, you hear footsteps outside your door. But when you get up to look, no one is there. Your dog or cat stares at something you can't see, and you think you hear voices in the next room. Suddenly you feel a chill in the air and hear a strange tapping sound. You're all alone, but it feels like someone is close by. Is it your imagination—or could it be something else? Could it be a ghost?

Throughout history people have reported these kinds of spooky feelings. Scary ghosts even appear in tales from ancient Rome and Greece. Could there be something behind the stories? Do the spirits of dead people really exist?

FACT Not all ghost reports are scary. Ghosts in some stories warn people of danger or help them find lost valuables. Sometimes they comfort people by showing them that there is life after death.

What was that spooky sound outside the door? Maybe it's time to call in the ghost hunters.

NEW WAYS TO INVESTIGATE

People have told ghost stories for thousands of years. Most stories were made up simply to give people a good scare. But a few stories may have had some truth to them. Even today many people believe in ghosts.

Until recently, people had few ways to research reports of ghostly activity. All they could do was spend some time in a reportedly haunted place. They would wait and watch—hoping to see or hear something unusual.

Today modern ghost hunters use advanced equipment to gather evidence of mysterious events. Their investigations often uncover natural causes that explain strange events. But sometimes ghost hunters find evidence that is difficult to explain.

evidence — information or items that prove something is true or false

Today's ghost hunters use modern equipment to research reports of ghosts.

CHAPTER 2

GHOST HUNTING TOOLS

Ghost hunters use many tools to conduct their investigations. One of the most useful tools is an ordinary camera. Sometimes strange things appear in pictures taken at places said to be haunted.

ORBS AND VORTEXES

Ghost hunters closely examine photos that contain images of unexplained objects. These objects were often not visible when the picture was snapped. The images sometimes appear as dark shadows or glowing mists. But more often they appear as round balls of light called orbs.

Glowing orbs are the most common type of unexplained image captured in photos. Some ghost hunters believe the orbs are ghosts trying to become visible. Others don't believe orbs are ghosts. They think the orbs are a type of mental or psychic energy that ghosts use to become visible.

Sometimes swirling funnels of light are seen in images. These strange funnels are called vortexes. Some ghost hunters think vortexes are single orbs moving at high speeds.

Orbs are often photographed in places reported to be haunted.

What the Skeptics Say

Skeptics are people who would like more proof that ghosts exist. They aren't convinced by the evidence ghost hunters gather. They know that camera flashes can reflect off dust or small insects to cause orbs. Orbs can also be caused by reflections of dirt or moisture on the lens. Skeptics also say vortex images are likely just camera straps that fall in front of the lens.

Skeptics point out that pictures of ghostly faces or figures can be faked. That's true. It's easy to add an image to a photo using a computer. Cameras that use film can also produce double exposures in a photo. Those double images can look just like ghostly figures.

Still, many ghost hunters don't believe all photos are fakes or accidents. They get excited when their cameras record something they did not see themselves.

skeptic — a person who questions things others believe in

There are several ways to create fake images of ghosts in photos.

Environmental Evidence

People often report feeling chilled in places said to be haunted. No one is sure why. Some people think a change in temperature is evidence of a spirit's presence. Ghost hunters often use `thermal` scanners and cameras to record temperature changes in haunted locations.

Heat is a form of energy. A few ghost hunters believe that ghosts might become visible by using energy from their surroundings. So if a haunted location suddenly becomes cold, it may mean a ghost is about to appear.

However, skeptics think there's nothing haunting about these chills. They say temperature changes are likely caused by drafts through old doors or windows. Another reason may be that the house is simply poorly heated.

Ghost hunters also take electromagnetic field (EMF) readings. Some people believe EMF readings jump when a ghost is nearby. But EMF readings are also high near TVs, computers, and electrical wiring. Skeptics often say that electronic equipment or bad wiring can cause unusual EMF readings.

Ghost hunters use thermal scanners and video recorders to gather evidence.

THE SOUNDS OF GHOSTS

Sometimes ghost hunters track spirits using audio recorders. Ghost hunters often capture strange sounds. In 1959 Swedish filmmaker Friedrich Jürgenson recorded birds singing on a tape recorder. When he played the tapes back, he believed he heard faint human voices.

Jürgenson experimented by setting the recorder up in different places. He heard even more strange voices. One sounded like his dead mother. Since then, audio recorders have become a popular tool to search for evidence of ghosts. Ghostly voices captured in the background of recordings are called electronic voice phenomena, or EVPs.

Skeptics think EVPs have logical explanations. They suspect strange audio recordings are caused by interference from radio or TV signals. But for many ghost hunters, EVPs are strong proof of a spirit's presence.

phenomena — unusual or remarkable events

Friederich Jürgenson recorded some of the first known EVPs.

Ghost hunters consider good EVPs some of their strongest evidence. Some EVPs are in sound ranges that are impossible for the human voice to make.

CHAPTER 3

GOING ON THE HUNT

How does a ghost hunt begin? Often, people are puzzled or frightened by unexplained activities. They may be curious about a strange sound or something they see. That's when they decide to contact a ghost hunting group.

ASKING QUESTIONS

Ghost hunters ask many questions before beginning an investigation. They listen closely to how a person answers. They need to decide if there could be a natural explanation for the person's story.

FACT A ghost hunter's first task is to decide if a person's report is serious. Some people might be taking illegal drugs or may be mentally unstable. They may believe they see or hear things that aren't really there.

People often imagine ghosts are active where none exist. A loose water pipe might be making banging sounds. A draft of cool air from an old window can cause a room to feel chilly. Older houses often make creaking sounds when they cool off at night. Ghost hunters usually look for these kinds of normal explanations first.

Ghost hunters often take scientific readings to rule out natural explanations first.

Gathering Clues

After ruling out possible natural explanations, ghost hunters begin gathering evidence. Part of the investigation includes researching a location's history. Ghost hunters look for clues about who may have lived or died there. This information will help them understand any evidence they might gather.

Ghost hunters usually work in teams to gather physical evidence. Each hunter has a different job. One person may take pictures. Another might shoot videotape. Others look for ghostly activity using EMF meters, audio recorders, and thermal scanners.

Ghost hunters do much of their work at night. They like working in quiet locations where they won't be disturbed. They also want to make sure the evidence they collect is not weakened by human activities. Ghost hunters also often use infrared cameras, which are more effective after dark.

infrared camera — a camera that locates objects by heat

A ghost hunter from the International Society for Paranormal Research takes scientific readings during an investigation.

Adding Up the Evidence

After gathering evidence for several hours, the ghost hunters pack up and leave. Then comes the most time-consuming part of the investigation. Team members closely examine film and photos to look for ghostly activity. They listen to hours of audio recordings for EVPs. Most of the time, the ghost hunters don't find anything unusual. Or the evidence they do find is not very convincing.

Sometimes, however, they discover something mysterious. A high EMF reading might be recorded at the same time a camera captures a strange image. Or perhaps an EVP captures a faint voice answering a ghost hunter's question. This kind of exciting evidence makes investigators eager for more hunts.

FACT During investigations, equipment and new batteries often go dead for no clear reason. Ghost hunters always make sure to carry extra batteries.

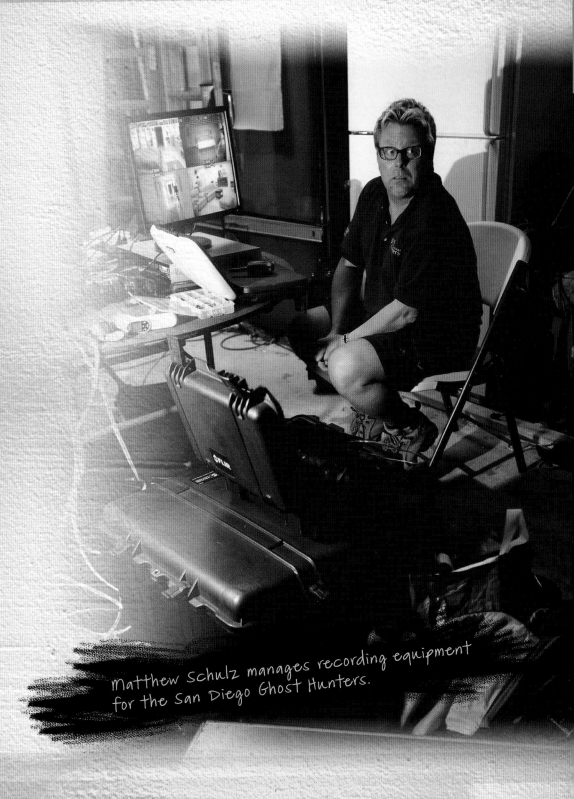

Matthew Schulz manages recording equipment for the San Diego Ghost Hunters.

CHAPTER 4

HUNTER TALES

Most people hunt ghosts out of curiosity and the thrill of the unknown. Hunters are fascinated when they find glowing orbs in a photo. And capturing moving objects or strange shadows on film can be very exciting. Whether or not they find strong evidence, ghost hunters often have interesting experiences during their investigations.

Chilling Orbs

L'Aura Hladik is the director of the New Jersey Ghost Hunting Society. One of her first cases stands out in her memory. Hladik was investigating a reported haunted house in Plainsboro, New Jersey. Late that night, Hladik was sitting on some stairs where a woman had fallen to her death. Suddenly, Hladik's right side began to feel cold.

Her husband took thermal readings on the stairs. The air temperature measured eight degrees cooler on Hladik's right side than on her left.

Her husband then took some pictures. The photos showed several glowing orbs clustered around her right side. Was this proof that the dead woman was haunting the stairs? It's impossible to know for certain. But it seemed to show that something strange was occurring at the house.

L'Aura Hladik

Natural Causes

Few investigations uncover interesting evidence. Much of the time, ghost hunters find common explanations for reported ghost activity. Ghost hunters Grant Wilson and Jason Hawes have learned that many reported ghosts aren't ghosts at all.

Wilson and Hawes are founders of The Atlantic Paranormal Society. The two investigators say that 80 percent of their cases turn up no evidence of paranormal activity. They've discovered that strange sounds are often just water pipes or furnace noises. In one case people felt a strange chill in a room. But the hunters discovered that the chill was caused by rags that were stuffed into the room's heating vents.

FACT
Ghost hunters sometimes sprinkle sugar or salt around objects supposedly moved by a ghost. It's an easy way to tell if an object has really been moved.

Jason Hawes (left) and Grant Wilson (right)

In another case, a couple reported banging noises, flickering lights, and screams from the attic. It sounded terrifying, but Wilson and Hawes discovered several natural explanations.

Squirrels had gotten into the home's walls, causing the loud thuds and banging sounds. The screams in the attic came from a hawk that had squeezed in through a heating vent. The hawk also caused the home's lights to flicker by brushing against a loose wire.

Grant and Hawes do believe that some ghost reports are real. But they enjoy proving reports have normal explanations. Of course, totally unexplainable cases are the most exciting cases of all.

Strange noises can often be traced back to a building's plumbing.

A Voice from Beyond

One of Hawes and Wilson's most memorable investigations took place at the home of a man whose grandfather had recently died. The ghost hunters didn't understand one of the EVPs they recorded. However, they became very excited when they learned that the man's grandfather was from Poland. The man told them that the words on the recording were in the Polish language.

Hawes and Wilson closely study recordings to look for signs of ghostly evidence.

A Ghostly Hand

American Paranormal Investigations has been hunting ghosts in Sacramento, California, since 2001. In 2006 they investigated a reportedly haunted motel and restaurant in Brookdale, California. Over several years people felt cold drafts and claimed they saw shadowy figures. TVs were said to turn on and off with no one around.

The ghost hunters captured several strange images with their cameras. One picture showed streaks and smears of light. Orbs were photographed at the same time that EMF detectors gave unusual readings. Meanwhile, both male and female voices were heard on EVPs.

After the investigators finished their work, they decided to relax. Suddenly, one of the ghost hunters said he felt a sharp pain rip through his body. Another hunter had been taking pictures of him at the same time. In one photo, a ghostly hand seemed to reach right through the ghost hunter's stomach!

Ghost hunters enjoy the challenge of solving ghostly mysteries.

LOVING THE UNKNOWN

Ghost hunters love getting to the bottom of ghostly mysteries. They enjoy gathering evidence that can be studied scientifically. And they enjoy discovering if there is more happening beyond people's imaginations. The mystery surrounding reported ghosts inspires ghost hunters to keep investigating the unknown.

GLOSSARY

apparition (ap-uh-RISH-uhn)—the visible appearance of a ghost

audio (AW-dee-oh)—having to do with how sound is heard, recorded, and played back

evidence (EV-uh-duhnss)—information, items, and facts that help prove something to be true or false

infrared camera (in-fra-RED KAM-ur-uh)—a camera that locates objects by the heat they give off

orb (ORB)—a glowing ball of light that sometimes appears in photographs taken at reportedly haunted locations

paranormal (par-uh-NOHR-muhl)—having to do with an unexplained event that has no scientific explanation

phenomena (fe-NOM-uh-nuh)—very unusual or remarkable events

psychic (SYE-kik)—having to do with a person's soul or mind

skeptic (SKEP-tik)—a person who questions things that other people believe in

thermal (THUR-muhl)—having to do with heat or holding in heat

READ MORE

Doak, Robin S. *Investigating Hauntings, Ghosts, and Poltergeists.*. Unexplained Phenomena. Mankato, Minn.: Capstone Press, 2011.

Shores, Lori, and illustrated by Eldon Doty. *Ghosts*. Truth and Rumors. Mankato, Minn.: Capstone Press, 2010.

Teitelbaum, Michael. *Ghosts and Real Life Ghost Hunters*. Mystery Files. New York: Franklin Watts, 2008.

INTERNET SITES

FactHound offers a safe, fun way to find Internet sites related to this book. All of the sites on FactHound have been researched by our staff.

Here's all you do:

Visit *www.facthound.com*

Type in this code: 9781429665179

 Check out projects, games and lots more at **www.capstonekids.com**

INDEX

American Paranormal
    Investigations, 28
apparitions, 11, 28
The Atlantic Paranormal
    Society, 24

electronic voice
    phenomena (EVP), 14,
      15, 20, 27, 28
equipment, 6, 20
    audio recorders, 14, 18
    cameras, 8, 10, 20, 23, 28
    electromagnetic field
      (EMF) meters, 13,
      18, 28
    infrared cameras, 18
    thermal scanners, 12, 18
    video recorders, 18

fake photos, 10

gathering evidence, 18, 20,
    24, 29

haunted locations, 6, 8,
    22, 28
Hawes, Jason, 24–27
Hladik, L'Aura, 22–23

Jürgenson, Friedrich, 14

Mumler, William, 23

natural explanations, 6, 10,
    12, 13, 14, 16, 17, 18, 24,
    26, 29
New Jersey Ghost Hunting
    Society, 22

orbs, 8–9, 10, 22, 23, 28

research, 6, 18

skeptics, 10, 12, 13, 14
strange noises, 4, 14, 16, 17,
    24, 26
studying evidence, 20, 29

temperature changes, 4, 12,
    17, 22–23, 24, 28

vortexes, 9, 10

Wilson, Grant, 24–27